Create
Your Own

Bling

By Ilene Baranowitz

@2007 by Ilene Baranowitz

Published by

krause publications

An Imprint of F+W Publications

700 East State Street • Iola, WI 54990-0001
715-445-2214 • 888-457-2873
www.krausebooks.com

Our toll-free number to place an order or obtain a free catalog is (800) 258-0929.

The following trademarked terms and companies appear in this publication:

Art Accentz™ Terrifically Tacky Tape™, B-D Foil-Wrapped Swabs, BeDazzler™, BeJeweler™ Stone Styler, BlingKits™, Bond™ 527, Brisk-Set, Crafter's Pick™ Jewel Bond™, Crystal Crafter®, Czech Preciosa®, Decorative Touch™, E-6000® Craft Adhesive, ebay®, GeMagic™, Gem-Tac™, Goodwill Industries International, Inc., Kandi Corp. Kandy Kane™, Mill Hill, Mylar®, PCStitch™, Rhinestone Pickerr-Uperr, Stitch Painter, Swarovski®, Teflon®, Valspar® Goof Off®, Wonder Tape™

Library of Congress Catalog Number: 2006925060

ISBN-13: 978-0-89689-437-2

ISBN-10: 0-89689-437-1

Designed by Heidi Bittner-Zastrow and Emily Adler

Edited by Erica Swanson

Acknowledgments

I'd like to thank the following:

Susan Ray, for being a terrific friend and connecting me with the wonderful people at F+W Publications.

Candy Wiza, for believing in my concept so much and championing it to the rest of the staff at F+W, and for all your help when things felt overwhelming.

Susan Sliwicki, for all your help during the transition between editors.

Sarah Brown, for your help in the initial stages of editing.

Erica Swanson, for being the greatest editor an author could want, and for stepping in when I really needed it most.

F+W Publications staff, illustrator and photographer for making this BLING come to life.

"Mister Nailhead" on eBay and Swarovski, Inc., for your help in making the projects a reality.

Abby Riba at Kandi Corporation, for your assistance with answers to many of my questions and your kind donations of materials.

Cochenille Design Studios for Stitch Painter, and M & R Technologies, Inc. for PC Stitch Pro.

Phil Brandt, the Rhinestone Guy, for the use of his fantastic color chart and all the wonderful rhinestone information available on his Web site.

Arthur Baker, for all of your help and encouragement always.

My parents, Alex and Thelma Kolotkin, for always being there for me in good times and bad

To my sister, Gayle, my brother-in-law, Marc, and Hunter, Gavin and Ciera — I love you all!

My sons, Linn and Logan, and their wives, Jill and Lena, for being the greatest family a mother could ask for — you make me so proud.

Garrett, my first grandson, born while the book was being written — I love you so much!

And mostly, my husband Dave — for being there for me and always believing in my crazy ideas.

Thanks,

Ilene

Table of Contents

Beginning to Bling!..........6

Sparkling Stones 7

Twinkling Tools..............14

Pretty Patterns.................24

Posh Purses 26

Crystal Contours Evening Bag...27

Polka Dot Purse...30

Lustrous Zigzag Bag..32

Radiant Red Clutch...36

Jewel Art Purse..40

Springtime Striped Handbag 43

Sparkling Seed Beads Bag...46

A-List Accessories...........49

Brilliant Business Card Case...50

Blossoms Lipstick Case 52

Curved Shell Coin Purse...55

Unforgettable Perfume Atomizer.....................................59

Glamorous Initialed Lighter 61

Updated Vintage Compact...64

Posh Pet Carrier..67

70.... Wow-Them Wearables

71.. Blazing Hot Sunglasses

73.. Ultimate BLING! Bracelet

75..Silver Starburst Shoes

77..Bow Barrette

79..Beautiful Lace Shawl

81................. High-Tech Toys

82..Encrusted iPod Case

85..Dazzling Cell Phone Case

87..Glittering Tape Measure

89.. Diabetes Monitor Case

91..Personalized Puppy Lead

93............. About the Author

94....................... Resources

Beginning to Bling!

Imagine yourself all decked out for a night on the town carrying a precious minaudière that you embellished yourself. You could turn heads wherever you go! That's what "Create Your Own Bling" is all about — teaching you how to design a dazzling new look that will make you feel like a Hollywood star.

Items encrusted with crystals and rhinestones are just as popular as ever. Judith Leiber, the grande dame of handbag design, has been creating jeweled handbags for four decades. Her bags command prices in the thousands — and they are worth every penny! Her purses are in the permanent collections of some of the finest museums, and she has designed for First Ladies, starlets, and the rich and famous. On the red carpet, there is an unwritten rule that designer gowns accented by million-dollar diamonds must be accompanied by a Judith Leiber purse. Those lucky enough to own one of her creations know that it is a prize to be cherished. These glistening status symbols can be found anywhere from runways to state dinners, and they are available in chic boutiques as well as high-end department stores.

My first encounter with a Judith Leiber purse was at an expensive department store in a very upscale shopping mall in Northern Virginia. You know the type of mall I mean — they are more like museums than retailers, and they might as well be museums because you can't afford to buy anything there! I was drawn to the purses displayed in a glass case, and their dazzling beauty took my breath away. From that day forward, I found myself going to the mall just to admire them — and the more I looked, the more crystal-embellished items I found.

To honor the creator of these masterpieces, I have adapted the technique of applying crystals to evening bags. If you have the patience for meticulously placing individual rhinestones on evening bags, you can fashion a beautiful satin treasure. Although these homemade accessories may not compare to the uniquely molded shapes and styles of Ms. Leiber's bags, usually referred to as minaudières, the effect can still be quite stunning. With a little imagination, you can find many vintage and current evening bags to decorate. Your bargain hunting skills will come in handy at thrift stores, flea markets, dollar stores and garage sales — and don't forget eBay!

In addition to evening bags, consider decorating other accessories — shoes, clothing, accessories such as compacts and lipstick holders, perfume bottles, pillboxes, mirrors, eyeglass frames and, of course, cell phones. The possibilities are endless!

I have become addicted to the thrill of the hunt and transforming my bargain finds into sparkling crystal studded creations — and I know you will love it too!

Sparkling Stones

Within the plethora of flat-backed crystals in all price ranges, from the brilliant Swarovski and Preciosa Austrian crystals to less expensive acrylic rhinestones, there are various sizes and a multitude of colors to meet your needs. In addition to crystals, there are flat-backed pearls and metal nail-heads in many colors, shapes, sizes and styles.

When choosing which rhinestones to use, bear in mind the expense of covering the desired item. It may look spectacular to cover the entire surface of a bag with Swarovski crystals, but those high-end stones may add up to an expensive endeavor. Check the color and size charts for ways to determine the quantity of stones you will need for any project.

Types of stones available:

• •● ●● Crystals ●●● •

Swarovski crystals

The name Swarovski has become almost synonymous with crystal flat-backs or rhinestones. The brilliance and clarity of the stones, due to the high lead content, provides the most spectacular bling of all the products on the market. The crystals are faceted with great precision, resulting in tiny prisms on the surface of the stones. Until recently, these crystals contained 12 facets surrounding the flat center panel on each stone. Swaroski recently introduced a new Xilion Rose cut with 14 facets, which add more brilliance and sparkle. In addition, the glue on the back of the hot-fix stones (application described on on page 15) melts at a lower temperature for faster application.

Czech Preciosa

These Austrian crystals are less expensive than their Swarovski counterparts, and there is some discussion among the various suppliers as to their value in different applications. Those who only deal with Swarovski tend to critique the Czech Preciosa stones, calling them inferior. However, those who carry both the Preciosa and Swarovski lines have a different opinion. These suppliers say that the Preciosas are just as bright — in fact, they are "flashier" from a distance of about two feet. The Czech Preciosa crystals are different because they have 8 facets instead of the 12 or 14 on Swarovski. There are some higher-facet count Czech Preciosa stones available, but they are more expensive. For now, each plane or cut is larger on the Preciosas, refracting more light over the entire surface. The Swarovskis have more cuts, and even though they refract less light, there are more cuts around the surface to provide more overall sparkle. Preciosa has recently revamped its cutting machines to provide a higher quality, and the company now concentrates even more on the fine quality of their AB Coatings. The Preciosas have a harder surface and will not break as readily as the Swarovski crystals, which makes them ideal for belts and collars.

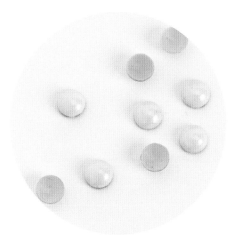

◦ ●◉ **Pearls** ◉●◦

Flatback pearls

Flatback pearls are half pearls that come in two different finishes: frosted and creamy bridal pearls. They can be glass, acrylic or metallic with a pearlized finish.

◦ ●◉ **Nailheads** ◉●◦

Nailheads

Nailheads come in a variety of sizes and shapes in metallic finishes. Some come with prongs for setting, and others are flatbacks adhered with hot-fix glue.

Rhinestuds

Beveled or faceted nailheads have colored metallic finishes that give the look of the glass due to the faceting but are much less expensive. From afar, they have sparkle and brilliance, but not as much as the true crystals.

◦ ●◉ **Acrylic** ◉●◦

Acrylic crystals

These inexpensive plastic rhinestones come in a variety of colors, shapes and sizes, starting at 5ss. These rhinestones do not have the sparkle and flash of the Swarovski or Preciosa crystals.

HFT

These transparent crystals have no foil or adhesive backs. The HFT stones can be used on glass and other transparent surfaces.

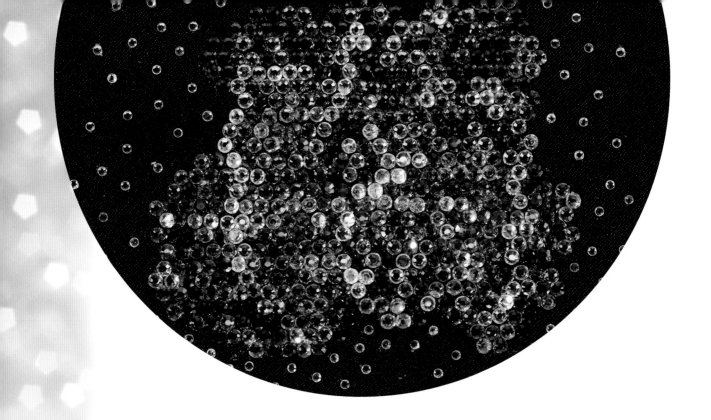

∘ ∘∘Colors∘∘ ∘

Classic Crystal Colors

These are the standard colors available from Swarovski and Czech Preciosa. The colors are comparable, but there are some differences between the companies' hues with the same color name.

AB Crystal Colors

AB Stands for Aurora Borealis, the colors of the Northern Lights. The coatings radiate beautiful oranges, yellows, blues and greens when viewed at different angles. The AB-coated stones are generally more expensive.

Swarovski Premium Crystal Colors

These are more recent colors that actually change color depending upon the light source. The colors are not created by a coating — it is the actual deeper, richer and varied colors of the glass itself.

Czech Preciosa Décor Colors

Décor is Preciosa's name for colors comparable to the Swarovski Premium Crystal Colors. Some of the stones are different colors, and sometimes they actually look different when the name and effect are supposed to be the same.

Swarovski Satin Crystal Colors

These stones do not refract light the way the other stones do — they are muted colors with a satin finish. They are appropriate for any application that requires a toned-down look. The Satin Crystal Colors appear darker and smokier because they pull the light in without reflecting as much.

The best way to decide which colors to use is to acquire a color chart. My favorite chart is produced by the Rhinestone Guy, Phil Brandt (you can order it online at www.rhinestoneguy.com). He applies one crystal of each color for both Swarovski and Czech Preciosa to a sheet of clear acetate with the corresponding name listed on the chart page below. In addition, he has placed one of each size stone across the top of the chart. The chart is worth everything you will pay for it if you plan to do much Blinging, because there is no way to capture the true colors on a printed book page or on a computer screen.

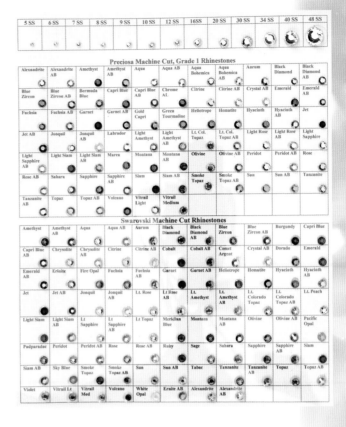

Common stone sizes

Stone Size (ss) vs. Millimeters (mm) vs. Pearl Plate (pp, only measured up to 16ss)

5ss	6ss	7ss	8ss	9ss	10ss	12ss	16ss
1.8mm	2.0mm	2.2mm	2.4mm	2.6mm	2.8mm	3.1mm	3.9mm
12pp	14pp	16pp	18pp	20pp	22pp	24pp	31pp

19ss	20ss	24ss	30ss	34ss	40ss	42ss	48ss
4.5mm	4.7mm	5.35mm	6.4mm	7.15mm	8.55mm	9.1mm	10.1mm

✿✿✿✿✿✿✿✿✿✿✿ TIPS ✿✿ •

Most stones are sold by the gross. One gross contains 144 pieces, or 12 dozen. One gross may sound like a lot, but coverage varies by size and placement.

25.5 mm = 1 inch

Stone coverage

How many stones do you need for your particular project? There's no easy answer. The best way to find out is to do a test.

1. Choose several stones in the size you plan to use.

2. Create a 1" square on a piece of paper.

3. Fill the square with the crystals in the manner in which you plan to complete your project — either Adjacent placement or Alternate placement, as described on pg. 24. Generally, you will need about ⅓ more stones for the Alternate placement.

4. Count the number of stones in your square — this is the number of stones per square inch. Now measure your project's length and height, and multiply this number to get the approximate number of square inches in the project. Multiply the number of square inches by the number of stones in your one-inch square. Then divide by 144, the total number in a gross of crystals, because most of the time you will be purchasing crystals by the gross.

If you are using one color, that's how many gross you will need. If you have two or more colors, figure roughly the proportion of colors — for example, ½ color one, ¼ color two and ¼ color three. That's all there is to it. Always plan on additional stones because they can drop on the floor or get misplaced, and there is always a chance that stones can fall off or break. So plan in advance and purchase the correct amount of stones for your project.

⊙ ⊙⊙ BlingKits ⊙ ⊙ ⊙ ⊙ ⊙ ⊙ ⊙ ⊙ ⊙ ⊙ ⊙

Each BlingKit contains Swarovski crystals, E-6000 adhesive, applicator syringes, wax sticks, stainless steel syringe tips, red adhesive syringe tips, crafting sticks, an instructional CD and a protective glove. This kit is a fairly complete and novel way of selling all of the materials needed if you decide to use the syringes and the E-6000 adhesive. Find it online at www.blingkits.com.

Alternatives to stones:

Montees

Montees are flatback crystals mounted in a setting with two perpendicular rows of holes on the back for stringing or wiring. This allows for some very exciting and creative possibilities.

Margaritas

These flower-shaped crystals have a hole drilled through the center from top to bottom. The best way to sew these onto your piece is to have the threaded needle come up through the fabric base, up through the center of the Margarita, then through a seed bead and back down through the Margarita center and into the fabric base, pulling the needle up through the center of the location of the next flower. These can also be glued to a surface with a seed bead glued into the center over the hole.

Crystal Seed Beads

These can be sewn on a project (see the Sparkling Seed Beads Bag on pg. 46) instead of glued. This is also a more economical alternative, and many crystal seed beads are available.

Chain Mounting

Chain mounting is a chain formed by attached individual metal mountings, which form a beautiful, flexible chain of cascading crystals.

Banding

Banding is plastic or elastic framework with crystals placed at regular intervals. This forms a strand of crystals that can be glued to the surface to follow the outline you intend to create. It is an easy way to apply a string of crystals to your project.

Mesh Mounting

Mesh mounting is a metal mesh to which the stones have been attached. The mesh is flexible and can be used to create beautiful bracelets, necklaces and banding. (See the Ultimate BLING! Bracelet on pg. 73.)

13

Twinkling Tools

Crystals are manufactured with a plain reflective backing and either a pre-glued or plain flat back. The plain backs are designed to be glued or set into one of the many prong-setting machines on the market.

Setters

Some setters work like a stapler — they push the prongs of the setting through the fabric from the back and clamp around the crystal to hold it in place. These setters should be used with paper and thin fabric.

Brisk-Set

The Brisk-Set can be adapted to attach round and oval settings as well as various nailheads and pearls. There are different adapters available for each type of application. The sturdy metal configuration of the Brisk-Set makes it a favorite of many who use these tools.

BeDazzler

This popular tool has been around since the 1980s, and it has gone through various modifications. It is made of plastic with a wheel on the base that rotates to accommodate the different size and style of settings, and comes with four heads.

GeMagic

The GeMagic looks and works like the BeDazzler with a few minor variations.

Prong-style stones

Simple Setter

This hand-held push-type setter is used in place of the staple-type setters mentioned above. Some people say that they are more accurate and easier to use, but this is just a personal preference.

Heat Setting

Heat-set rhinestones can be applied with a special tool designed for this purpose. Several are available (including the Kandi Kane Hot-Fix Applicator, which is my personal favorite), or you can apply the stones with an iron or a heat press.

Heat-setting tools melt the glue on the backs of the pre-glued hot-fix stones. The various wands heat the individual stones one at a time to a temperature of 290-300 degrees. After approximately 25 to 30 seconds of sufficient pressure, the stone is secured to the surface. Most fabrics, such as polyester, nylon, denim and silk, work well with such applications, but acrylic and acetate are not suitable for hot-fix. Test the fabric you will use beforehand, because there are no guarantees that any particular fabric will work. Heat-set stones can also be used on paper and some craft items by attaching them with the heat-set tool. Do not use the hot-fix technique for leather, glass, ceramics or metal.

Heat-set tools come with an assortment of tips, which fit over most flatbacks. Use the next size up if the tip won't fit over the stone. The tools also come with a stand to rest the hot tool on while you are working.

Heat-Set Tools

Kandi Kane

The Kandi Kane is the most popular, top of the line, new and improved model designed for crafters and hobbyists of all types.

Professional Touch

This is Kandi's brand-new professional version, which now includes an on/off switch. It also has a more ergonomic design.

Crystal Crafter

The Crystal Crafter is Kandi Corp.'s original model for general use.

Decorative Touch

The Decorative Touch is similar to the Kandi Kane. It is a top-of-the-line model designed for sewing, quilting and fiber crafts.

BeJeweler Stone Styler

This setter is similar to the Kandi Kane but manufactured by a different company. It was created specifically for affixing Swarovski crystals.

Other Methods

Iron

Use a dry iron with no holes in the sole plate.

Commercial T-shirt appliqué presses

These are available at T-shirt shops across the country. For a price, you might be able to get them to apply your appliqué for you.

Transfer sheets

When using an iron or a large T-shirt press, transfer sheets make it easy to place and press. Use special Mylar transfer sheets designed for this purpose. Place the sheet over your design or grid, sticky side up. Place the stones face down, and remember to set letters and specific directional designs backwards, because you will turn it upside down to apply. Use only heat-set stones for this purpose.

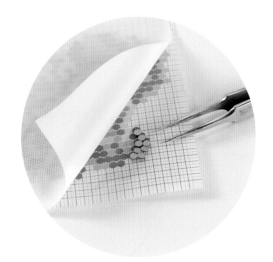

Applying a heat-set transfer

Materials

- Heat-set stones
- Tweezers
- Mylar transfer sheet

- Iron or T-shirt press
- Muslin or Teflon sheet

1. Examine the transfer to make sure that all of the stones are in the proper position. Fix any mistakes with a pair of tweezers. This is the time to make corrections, because once applied, the stones are permanent.

2. Place the project on an ironing board without padding. Peel the backing from the tape on the transfer, and place the transfer on the item to be embellished face up with the glue backs on the item's surface.

3. Place a Teflon sheet or a piece of muslin over the top of the transfer. The sheet will be held in place by the transfer's tacky backing. Set the iron — preferably one with no steam holes — to medium or wool, and place it straight down on the transfer. Do not move the iron around. Hold it there for 25 to 30 seconds. If you use a large heat press, set the pressure to approximately 15 lbs.

4. Let the piece cool for only a few seconds before removing the tape. The tape needs to be removed while it's still warm, but not too hot to touch, or it will stick.

5. Test to be sure that the stones are attached securely by prodding them very gently. If they lift off of the project, press again for another 25 to 30 seconds.

TIP

Do not dry clean any item that you BLING.

Adhesives

Glues and super-strong tapes work very well for applying rhinestones that do not have adhesive backs. You can also glue heat-set rhinestones to surfaces that are incompatible with the adhesive on the stones, such as metal or leather.

Glues

Gem-Tac and Jewel Bond are water-based products that do an excellent job. They were designed for adhering the stones to fabrics, but they work just as well on most other surfaces. These glues cannot be frozen, as the stones will pop off with prolonged exposure to the extreme cold.

E-6000 Craft Adhesive, Epoxy Glue and Bond 527 are permanent glues. These compounds are caustic, so be careful with these products. All should be used with rubber gloves in well-ventilated areas.

TIP

Do NOT use
hot-melt or instant glue

Applying stones with glue:

You can apply the glue to either the stones or the project. To apply the glue to the stone, put the glue on the back of each stone and place it on the project. You must put enough glue on the stone to cover the back completely. Apply with a toothpick or a syringe. Or, place a small area of glue on the actual project. Don't use too much glue at one time, or it will dry before you can affix the stones. Apply a thin, smooth layer with a brush or a toothpick.

⚬ ◉◉◉ Materials ◉

- ◉ Glue
- ◉ Stones of your choice
- ◉ Rubbing alcohol and cotton balls, or alcohol pads (such as B-D foil-wrapped swabs)
- ◉ Old CD

- ◉ Short-nap paintbrush and glass of water for rinsing
- ◉ Toothpicks
- ◉ ALTERNATE: Syringe

Ready, Set, Bling!

1. Rub the project's surface with alcohol to remove any grime before applying the stones.

2. Use a short-nap paintbrush and toothpicks to apply the glue. An old CD makes a great surface for the glue. Dip the brush in the glue, and apply to the back of each stone or to the surface of the project.

⚬◉◉◉ TIP ◉◉◉⚬

To use a syringe, fill it with glue and use a glue applicator tip.

Removing Glue

Use acetone or Goof Off to remove excess E-6000, Epoxy Glue and Bond 527. Be careful, because acetone can be dangerous. Water removes Gem-Tac or Jewel Bond, and any of the orange or citrus-based cleaning products also work very well for removing water-based glues. If you need to get rid of extra glue, do so shortly after applying.

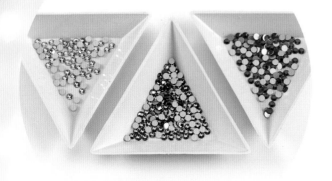

Tape

Terrifically Tacky Tape and Wonder Tape

These tapes are very strong — in fact, they are probably the strongest and most reliable tapes on the market. They will hold the stones on different hard surfaces, and there won't be any signs of glue around the edges. It is difficult to remove stones from the tape if you try. Use tape for flat, regular shapes without curved surfaces.

Other Tools

Sorting Trays

Sorting trays make it easy to organize and sift stones. Pour approximately ½ gross of one color of the stones into each tray at a time, leaving one tray empty. You will need most of the stones to be right side up for easy application. When you run out of stones that are right side up, shift the tray from side to side like you are panning for gold. You will be surprised to see how many shift correctly when you do this. Another way to get more to turn right side up is to move the stones from one tray to the empty extra tray and start working from that tray. When I get down to the last few stones that don't want to turn, I use the second tray method. Whatever you do, don't get obsessed with having all the stones right side up all the time.

Rhinestone Pickerr Uperr

Use this tool, a homemade applicator stick or a pair of tweezers to place stones on the project. The Rhinestone Pickerr Uperr is a handy tool I purchased from a beauty supplier. They are used for applying stones to manicured nails, but they work perfectly for our purposes. There are different size applicators on each end of the stick with a substance that adheres briefly to the stone, allowing you to transfer it from your sorting tray to the project. You can also use a toothpick or a lollipop stick and add a dollop of dental wax formed into a point with your fingers. Either of these two applicators requires you to place the stone on the project with the tip of the stick and then twist the stick between your fingers to release the stone. This motion becomes automatic after a few placements. You can also use a pair of tweezers to pick up the stones.

Removing stones

If you are careful, you can remove stones with a pair of tweezers, but it is difficult to remove them successfully. If you are pulling stones off fabric, you can create a hole with the tweezers; if you are removing stones from a metal surface, it can scratch. So, removing stones without marring the project is a very difficult task.

In addition to potentially damaging the project, you may also break the stones themselves. The separation of the stones from the mirrored backings can leave the stones de-mirrored, so the surface from which it was removed may have a shiny silver spot. If the stones are reapplied with the mirroring removed, the reflected color will appear darker and uneven.

Beaded Chains

Beaded chains can turn an ordinary accessory into a fabulous piece of Bling. Breaking the design of the chain down into manageable sections makes beading easier and takes the angst out of creating any beautiful beaded item. Use beaded chains to accentuate purses or bags covered in BLING!

Materials

- .019 or .024 heavyweight coated beading wire (21 or 49 strand preferably, for strength and flexibility)
- Crimp beads and pliers
- Assorted beads in colors to coordinate with your flat-backed crystals
- 3mm gold- or silver-tone filler beads
- Bead board or cushioned bead mat to prevent loose beads from rolling
- Purse with purchased chain or strap removed (leave loops to attach beaded chain)

Ready, Set, Bling!

1. Decide on the finished length of your chain, and cut the beading wire 5" to 6" longer. This will allow for the extra length of the tails needed to secure the chain to the purse or bag.

2. To create a pattern for the chain, choose one bead as your center focal bead. Arrange additional beads on the bead mat or bead board on either side of the center bead, in the same order on each side. I like to add a small 3mm silver-tone or gold-tone round bead between each bead in the chain — this gives a more finished, unified look, since it pulls all the beads together consistently with the same shape, size and color between every bead on the chain.

3. In this manner, create a single 2" to 4" section that can be repeated several more times around the entire length of the chain.

4. Create a second section of beads the same way you created the first section. All the beads on the strand should relate to one another, either as a single color or as a color scheme with 2 or 3 colors pulled from the bag.

5. Using multiple repeats of the one or two sections you designed above, alternate these sections until you reach the desired length, starting and ending with the same section between the two sides of the chain for balance.

6. String one crimp bead on the cut strand of beading wire, take the longer end through the loop attached to the bag, and then run the long end back through the crimp bead. To secure the cord to the bag, leaving about 1½" to 2" of cord on the short side, slide the crimp bead close to the loop on the bag, and crimp the bead, checking that the ends of the cord are crimped securely.

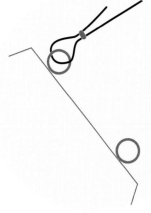

Step 6

7. Start adding the beads to the long length, stringing the first few beads over both ends of the long and short cords until the short end is hidden inside all the beads strung to that point.

8. When you have strung all of the beads, check to make sure that no beads were inadvertently left out of your pattern, and then thread another crimp bead on the end. Run the cord through the other connecting loop on the opposite side of the bag. Then, run the cord back through the crimp bead and through the next several beads. Pull the cord tight — this will push the crimp bead up against the connector loop to the bag and leave the strand tightly strung. When it is fairly tight, crimp the crimp bead, and cut the cord close to the bead from which it is exiting, completing the beaded chain.

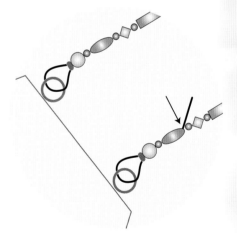

Step 8

 # Pretty Patterns

Grids

I have included two different types of grids for your use. Print these on clear transparency film, or take them to a print shop to have them do it for you. You can then take either grid and place it over your design. You will be able to apply the stones by following the number of circles on your grid. You might want to temporarily attach the transparency to your design and then work from that so it won't slip.

Adjacent

Stones are placed next to each other in even rows going across and up and down. Watch the rows to make sure that they are all even.

Alternate

Stones are round, so in this configuration, stones fit between the stones of the previous row. The first row lines up with the third row, and the second row lines up with the fourth row. This provides for a tighter fit and uses 1/3 more stones than the Adjacent pattern.

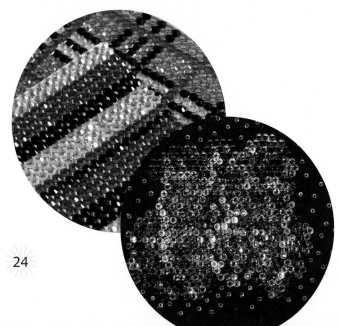

Adjacent Grid pattern

Alternate Grid pattern

Ideas for Creating Patterns

Design sources are all around us. This book includes patterns for you to follow, but don't stop there — look for pattern sources in coloring books, stained glass patterns, quilt block patterns, clip art and rubber stamp designs. Or, use one of the needlework programs to help you plan your pattern.

PCStitch or Stitch Painter

These needlework programs available for the computer can be used to create patterns from your designs. You can scan in your picture, and it will give you a grid that you can print out. Just use your colors in place of the embroidery threads to fill your pattern.

Working on Patterns

A magnetic board designed for reading counted cross-stitch patterns is an excellent tool to use for copying patterns. The magnets line up the line and location to mark your place, and they move easily as the pattern progresses.

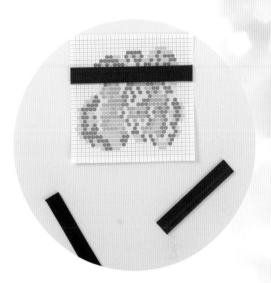

Where to find items to Bling!

eBay

Your attic

Thrift stores

Goodwill Industries

Consignment shops

Antique stores

Department or outlet stores

Flea markets

Garage sales

Dollar stores

Discount stores

Shoe stores

Handbag or jewelry outlets

Posh Purses

Crystal Contours
Evening Bag

Objective:

 Outline with crystals, keeping rows and columns straight.

I needed an evening bag for my son's wedding. When I found this bag, I knew that I would have something very special if I added crystals. This was the beginning of a brand-new world for me, one that would be dazzling like the crystals I would use! Okay, so I tend to get a bit carried away — but the images in my mind sparkle when I talk about my new passion!

The bag's shape attracted my eye. I decided to run three rows of larger crystals (20ss) side by side, following the contours of the purse. This technique can be used anytime you like the shape of a purse and wish to outline the curves. It's simple and elegant!

◦ ◦◉ Materials ◉ ◦ ◉ ◦ ◉ ◦ ◉ ◦ ◉ ◦ ◉ ◦ ◉ ◦ ◉ ◦ ◉ ◦ ◉ ◦ ◉ ◦ ◉

- ◉ 2 gross clear 20ss Swarovski heat-set crystals
- ◉ 1 gross clear AB 20ss Swarovski heat-set crystals
- ◉ Kandi Kane Heat-Set Applicator

- ◉ Black satin evening bag with curved closure
- ◉ ALTERNATE APPLICATION — use foil-backed crystals with Gem-Tac or Jewel Bond

◦ ◦◉ TIP ◉ ◦ ◦ ◦

It's all visual — trust your eye for straight placement, but if you need to check for evenness, use a straight edge or ruler along the top and sides of each row.

Ready, Set, Bling!

1. Starting at the back bottom corner, build rows consisting of 1 clear, 1 AB and 1 clear crystal. Place them side-by-side, working along the border, up the back of the bag, across the rounded flap and back down the other side of the back. Try to keep the three crystals lined up next to each other while keeping the column of crystals straight. This should be easier to accomplish on the straight sections, but it will require some careful spacing as the rows progress around the curve.

2. Place the crystals on the inside of a curve closer together, and place the crystals radiating out around the curve farther apart. Keeping the rows aligned will pay off when you are lining up with the other straight back edge.

3. When you come close to the bottom of the back, begin to space out the remaining rows so that the bottom will appear visually even on each side. The last row should line up with the first row on the opposite side.

4. Use the same technique for working the contour of the front edges.

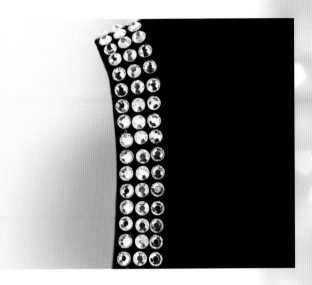

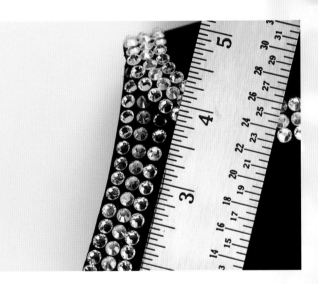

Polka Dot Purse

Objective:

To camouflage a printed silver faux-rhinestone pattern by placing real crystals on the bag, giving it a lovely new look.

This bag was very attractive, with a printed fabric of shiny silver holographic dots on a white background. As nice as the purchased bag was, I felt that the dots needed something more. The solution was to add Aqua crystals — what an easy and beautiful transformation!

❀ ❀❀ Materials ❀❀ ❀

- ❀ 1 gross aquamarine (or color of your choice)
- ❀ 12ss Swarovski heat-set crystals
- ❀ Kandi Kane Heat-Set Applicator
- ❀ Silver satin evening bag
- ❀ ALTERNATE APPLICATION — use foil-backed crystals with Gem-Tac or Jewel Bond glue with flat brush or toothpicks.

Ready, Set, Bling!

1. Adhere one crystal over each spot, checking that they are centered as you fill the entire surface with crystals.

Before

Blinged!

Lustrous Zigzag Bag

Objective:

To convert a beaded version of a bargello needlepoint pattern to a pattern specific to crystal application and center it on a panel; to conserve the cost of crystals while still completely covering a prominent section of the purse; and to replace the attached chain with a hand-beaded strap.

The shape of this evening bag lent itself to filling the center panel completely, thereby avoiding covering the black side panels with additional crystals. This provides a lot of bling for the buck while creating an elegant, runway-ready purse. This bag was sold as a promotional holiday item bundled with perfume by one of the major cosmetic companies. These promotions are common — so why not take advantage of the accessories and frost them with crystals?

Materials

- 2 gross aquamarine 12ss Swarovski heat-set crystals
- 2 gross tanzanite 12ss Swarovski heat-set crystals
- 2 gross jet black 12ss Swarovski heat-set crystals
- Kandi Kane Heat-Set Applicator
- Disappearing ink pen
- Converted bargello needlepoint pattern
- Materials for beaded chain, if desired (see page 22)
- Black satin bag
- ALTERNATE APPLICATION — use foil-backed crystals with Gem-Tac or Jewel Bond glue and brush or toothpicks.

Ready, Set, Bling!

1. Measure the widest part of the center panel. Find the center of the pattern, and then measure out equally on each side of the center to find the total width of the pattern.

2. To create a straight line across, measure down both sides from the top equally, and mark with the disappearing ink pen. Draw a line across the row, intersecting the marked points you have measured. This will be your guide for the first row, which should be straight across and level with the bottom of the bag.

3. After counting the number of crystals in each color, place them side by side on the guideline across the bottom of the center panel. To find the center crystal in the pattern, divide the guideline in half. Start by adhering the crystal in the color corresponding to the center color on your pattern sheet to the center point you have marked.

4. Working from the center crystal on the guideline, add the corresponding colors in your pattern on either side of the center.
NOTE: There will be an odd number of crystals on each line, with an equal number on each side and one crystal in the center.

5. Build upon the base row using Adjacent placement, adding crystals by following the printed chart. Count the number of crystals corresponding to those in the pattern and adhere them in line vertically with the crystal on the row below. Check the pattern as it builds to see that the crystals are placed correctly, watching for vertical and horizontal alignment. You might want to use a ruler or straight edge to check.

6. When you reach the point where the sides of the panel taper and you can no longer fit the two crystals on either end, simply reduce the length of the pattern line, being sure to remove one crystal from each side and place the first crystal directly over the SECOND crystal in the pattern. Work across. Repeat this each time you run out of room on the sides due to the tapering of the panel.

7. The sample purse came with a wrist-length, silver-blackened chain. If you are not happy with the supplied chain, consider replacing it with a beaded strand (see page 22).

Zigzag pattern

Radiant Red Clutch

Objective:

To cover an entire surface with crystals, as inspired by a Judith Leiber original, and to obtain the desired look without going into debt.

I started this project with great expectations. I planned to cover the purse completely with 12ss Siam Swarovski crystals in a tight Alternate row pattern. However, after I had applied 8 gross of premium Swarovski crystals, the project was no more than 1/3 complete. Anticipating the need for approximately 16 additional packages, I knew that this would be not only out of my league financially, but it would also be an impractical project for this book. I was ready to scrap the entire bag and move on to the next project, but the cost of the eight packages I had already used aggravated me.

After two days of staring at this botched project, I decided to try to reclaim the crystals, even if it meant forfeiting the bag.

I was able to remove the stones I had already applied, and I decided the basic bag could still be salvaged. I could cover it with larger, less expensive rhinestones placed slightly farther apart in even, Adjacent rows, rather than the tighter Alternate rows that eat up more stones per square inch. Wherever the placement of the larger rhinestones revealed a tear or silver spot, I added smaller 12ss Siam crystals.

The whole process accomplished two things: I was able to salvage the purse, and I found a less expensive alternative to pass on to you. Hopefully it will be inspiration for the possibility that you will run into a similar situation — take heart and don't give up!

Materials

- 6 gross clear 20ss flat-backed crystal or acrylic rhinestones — foil-backed or heat-set
- 4 gross Siam 12ss Swarovski foil-backed or heat-set crystals (or less expensive glass or acrylic foil-backed or heat-set rhinestones)
- Crystal costume jewelry brooch
- 1/8" gold metallic cording

- Disappearing ink pen
- Flexible tape measure
- Ruler
- Materials needed to create a beaded chain, if desired (see pg. 22)
- Gem-Tac
- Oval red satin purse

Ready, Set, Bling!

1. Draw a straight line with the disappearing ink across the center of the bag after taking measurements to be sure that the line is straight and level. Use a flexible tape measure to wrap around the curves and measure an equal amount from the bottom rim (in this case, 3" from the bottom), placing several dots at the 3" mark. Then use a ruler or straight edge to draw a line across to use as the base row.

2. Adhere one 20ss clear rhinestone on the line. Take another rhinestone and place it next to this one, but do not glue it down. Use this second rhinestone only for spacing the next rhinestone that you will adhere to the purse. This spacing does not have to be tight — the looser the spacing, the fewer stones you will use overall. Just be consistent throughout the project! Remove the loose rhinestone and place it next to the second glued stone, again without gluing this one, and adhere another rhinestone next to this loose one. Repeat across the row.

3. Using a straight edge lined up next to the glued row, draw a line just above the first with the disappearing ink. Use this line as a guide for placing the rhinestones on the next row.

4. Place the rhinestones in line with the empty spaces in the row below, alternating the placement of rhinestones and blank spaces on each line. Completely cover the purse in this manner — the curve along the edges will affect the precision of the spacing.

5. When completed, apply one 12ss Siam stone between each larger rhinestone.

6. To finish the purse, adhere the gold metallic cord around the rim. The cord gives the purse a finished, sophisticated look. This embellishment was modeled after Judith Leiber's purses. Don't be afraid to use an inspiration to ignite your own creative expression!

7. You can choose to decorate the flap with additional crystals. In this example, six 20ss clear crystals were placed in a circle with one additional crystal in the center. 12ss Siam crystals were interspersed around them.

8. Bead a chain, if desired (see pg. 22).

TIP

Covering the entire surface on a large area will still result in some spacing irregularities — that's because it is hand-crafted, and it is part of the charm of doing it yourself! So don't beat yourself up if it's not perfect. My example wasn't perfect, either, but I found a way to mask the imperfections. I took a crystal brooch that I haven't worn for years and pinned it on the front of the bag, covering any irregularities in the rhinestone placement.

Jewel Art Purse

Objective:

 To place a picture composed entirely of crystals on the center front panel of a purse.

After getting somewhat shell-shocked by my ambitious attempt to cover the entire surface of an evening bag, I was ready for a design that would not require a major investment in crystals. One of the objectives of this book is to help you get the greatest Bling for your buck, and this project is an attempt to do just that. Not filling the entire front panel saved many square inches of coverage, along with the savings in the cost of crystals.

However, once the pattern application was completed on the bag, it still looked like something was missing. Scattering tiny 5ss clear crystal pinpoints over the remainder of the front added an enchanting twinkle and brought the finished design to life!

Materials

- 1 gross emerald 12ss Swarovski heat-set crystals
- 1 gross peridot 12ss Swarovski heat-set crystals
- 1 gross tanzanite 12ss Swarovski heat-set crystals
- 1 gross aquamarine 12ss Swarovski heat-set crystals
- 1 gross amethyst 12ss Swarovski heat-set crystals
- 1 gross clear 12ss Swarovski heat-set crystals
- 1 gross clear 5ss Swarovski heat-set crystals

- Kandi Kane Heat-Set Applicator
- Pattern or other picture of choice to convert, actual size
- Clear alternating row grid
- Disappearing ink pen
- Black satin evening bag with flat front at least 6" x 6"
- ALTERNATE APPLICATION — use foil-backed crystals with Gem-Tac or Jewel Bond glue applied with brush or toothpicks.

Ready, Set, Bling!

◦ ◦ ◦◦ TIP ◦◦ ◦ ◦

It is best to find the center of the template and place that first dot at the beginning of a row in the center, where the pattern is the widest. You can then work up from that row and when the top half is completed, come back to the first row and work down until the entire pattern is finished.

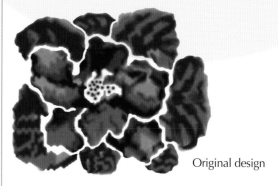

Original design

1. Lay your clear copy of the grid on top of the full-size picture to convert. Make a color copy, or scan and print the two together. Cut the printout closely, following the outline of the design and leaving a thin white border around your template.

2. Place the artwork in its desired location on the bag. Holding your template to the surface, lift one corner and draw a dot at the beginning of one of the rows. This is where you will place a crystal. Measure from the bottom of the bag to the dot you drew, and use the same measurement to place additional points across. Then, draw a line through all the points with the disappearing ink. Use the original spot that you drew at the beginning of the row to start building the pattern.

3. To facilitate accurate placement according to the pattern, it may be easier to fold the template under the row you are filling. When you complete the row, fold the template under and work the next row. Use this method to complete all rows. If you start at the center of the pattern where the rows are widest, unfold the template when you have finished the first half and turn both the bag and the template in order to work the rest of the pattern upside down from the starting row.

4. Randomly affix tiny clear 5ss crystals over the rest of the unadorned area.

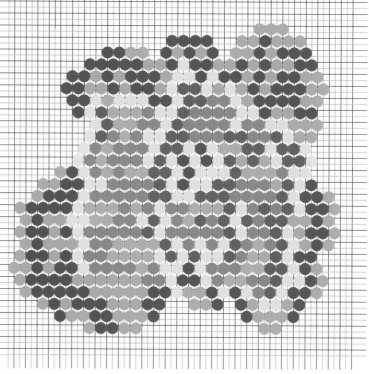

Flower grid

Blinged!

Springtime Striped Handbag

Objective:

To create a striped pattern out of crystals, and to sew or glue alternative shapes and types of crystals on a project.

I found this fabulous green satin evening bag, and I knew that I had to embellish it with BLING! A simple purse covered with crystals is magical, and this bag is no exception. I used the Margarita beads to decorate the edge of the flap and accented each one with a Delica bead in the center. These can be sewn on or they can be glued (which I chose to do in this case). Instead of using glue to attach the crystals, you may use Terrifically Tacky Tape — it's up to you.

Materials

- 5 gross peridot 12ss Swarovski foil-backed crystals
- 5 gross light rose 12ss Swarovski foil-backed crystals
- 4 gross clear 12ss Swarovski foil-backed crystals
- 36 peridot Swarovski Margarita (flower) beads
- 36 light rose Delica seed beads, or other size 11 seed beads
- Bead needle and thread (optional)
- GemTac or Jewel Bond glue
- Flat brush or toothpicks for spreading glue
- Terrifically Tacky Tape
- Peridot satin evening handbag

TIP

ALTERNATE METHOD: Glue the crystals onto the bag, following the striped pattern — see directions in the front of the book for this application method.

Ready, Set, Bling!

1. Glue or sew the row of Margaritas along the edge of the flap. If glued, do not add the Delicas until the rest of the project is done. To sew them on, run the needle with thread through the single layer of satin, up through the center of the margarita, through one Delica bead and back down through the hole in the Margarita and into the satin. Come up at the center of the next Margarita bead and repeat around the flap.

2. To decorate the purse, cut a piece of tape to the size and dimension of the purse flap. Peel back one small corner of the back of the tape. Place the unpeeled or non-sticky part of the tape to line up with the project. When it is properly placed, touch the part that has been peeled back to the satin bag, and slowly remove the rest of the backing from the back of the tape, pressing it down in place and smoothing as you go.

3. Remove only a single row of the top layer of the tape protective paper at a time, and place the crystals down on the exposed tape, following the pattern. Continue until the entire pattern is finished.

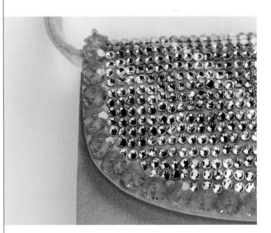

Sparkling
Seed Beads Bag

Objective:

 To create BLING without the expense of flat-back crystals by using bead embroidery.

I was inspired by a beautiful book, "Bead Embroidery — the Complete Guide" by Jane Davis. Seed beads are a terrific alternative for anyone who wants to have BLING on a budget. These crystal seed beads have a sparkle that can simulate the look of Swarovski crystals. They are not quite the same, of course, but they still provide a gratifying end result.

Materials

- #10 plastic canvas for embroidery
- #11 seed beads, Mill Hill Crystal Ice
- Bead needles — preferably large eye needles to facilitate threading
- Silver metallic embroidery thread
- Gem-Tac or Jewel Bond glue
- Star pattern or pattern of your choice
- PCStitch or Stitch Painter software (optional)
- Magnetic stitch counter
- Black satin purse with a large, flat front

Ready, Set, Bling!

1. Using the pattern provided or one of your own plotted out on graph paper or in a computer embroidery program, cut the embroidery canvas to fit the design exactly. Be very careful to include the correct number of holes for each stitch, and then smooth the cut edges so it doesn't catch the thread during embroidery. It is easier to do this up front, because you won't have to cut threads straying beyond the border of the design once the entire project is completed.

2. Place the chart on a magnetic stitch counter to keep your place while you are working. You can move the magnets as you go, which makes it very easy to find your way through the pattern. Following your chart, fill the canvas with beads, placing one bead for each embroidery stitch. Leave the blank spaces empty, or if you prefer, use a different color to fill them. Either way, the pattern will begin to emerge as you create it.

3. When you are finished, glue the entire canvas to the front of the bag, being careful to keep it straight. Use enough glue to cover the entire back without spreading to the rest of the satin on the bag.

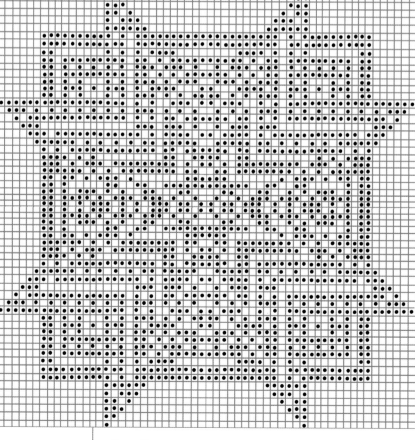

Star pattern

A-List Accessories

Brilliant Business Card Case

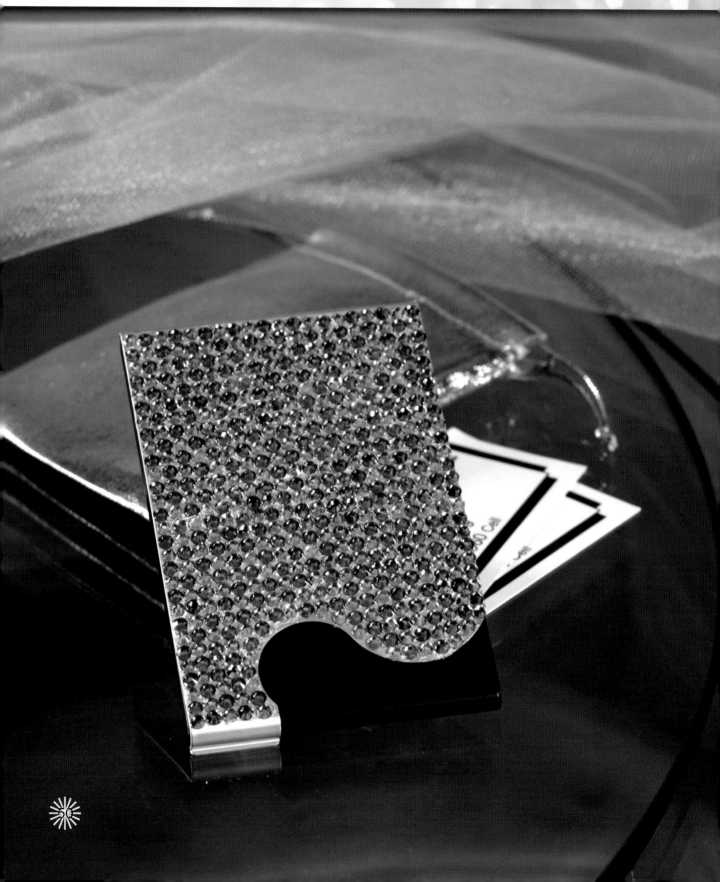

Objective:

To cover the entire surface of an item by alternating two colors side by side.

When you meet a new business acquaintance, first impressions are crucial, and you want to express your professionalism with style and flair. Pulling out a fabulous crystal-encrusted cardholder will have "shock and awe" value and show your new contact that you are confident and sophisticated — in other words, you are someone with whom they will want to associate. Little will they know how easy it was to create this spectacular look!

❂ ❂❂ Materials ❂❂ ❂

- ❂ Alcohol swab, or rubbing alcohol and cotton
- ❂ 1 gross aqua 12ss Swarovski foil-back crystals
- ❂ 1 gross tanzanite 12ss Swarovski foil-back crystals
- ❂ Gem-Tac or Jewel Bond glue
- ❂ Plain metal business card case

❂ ❂❂ TIP ❂❂ ❂

For a different look, use a plaid or striped pattern instead.

Ready, Set, Bling!

1. Clean case with alcohol swab.

2. Apply crystals in Adjacent rows, alternating one aqua and one tanzanite crystal. Fill the entire surface with crystals, fitting them into the curved area in the same pattern of side-by-side alternating colors.

3. Periodically check for even placement by placing a ruler or straight edge along both the horizontal and vertical rows.

Blossoms Lipstick Case

Objective:

 To cover a surface completely by using random placement rather than a grid, and to create a flower out of crystals.

This little lipstick case can hold two regular tubes of lipstick. Since it fits nicely in the palm of your hand, use it for an evening out to hold a single tube of lipstick, a key and some change.

This Asian floral print case was purchased at a local Chinese restaurant. It just goes to show that you never know where you'll find your next inspiration to create glamorous bling!

◦ ◉ ◉ Materials ◉

- ◉ 2 gross cobalt 12ss Swarovski heat-set crystals
- ◉ 1 package 48 count fuchsia 12ss Swarovski heat-set crystals
- ◉ 1 package 48 count light Colorado topaz 12ss Swarovski heat-set crystals
- ◉ 1 package 48 count clear AB 12ss Swarovski heat-set crystals

- ◉ 1 package 48 count clear 5ss Swarovski heat-set crystals
- ◉ Kandi Kane Heat-Set Applicator
- ◉ Materials for beaded wrist strap, if desired (see pg. 22)
- ◉ Small lipstick case
- ◉ ALTERNATE APPLICATION — use foil-backed crystals with Gem-Tac or Jewel Bond glue with brush or toothpicks.

Ready, Set, Bling!

1. Begin by making the flowers. Use fuchsia and light Colorado topaz crystals to create 5 petals, and adhere them to the case. Glue one clear AB 12ss crystal in the center of each flower. Fill all of the flowers on the front in the same manner, using different colors to coordinate with the colors on the fabric.

2. Once all of the flowers are finished, fill in the background with the cobalt crystals. Place the cobalt stones randomly on the case, because the room between the flowers will vary. There will undoubtedly be small spaces left around some of the crystals, so fill these blank holes with the tiny clear 5ss stones. Scatter them around the entire pattern.

3. If desired, create a beaded wrist strap and attach it around the back hinge.

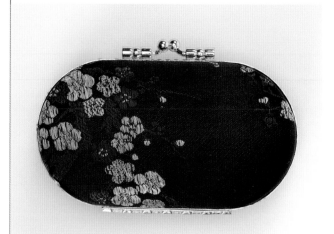

Before

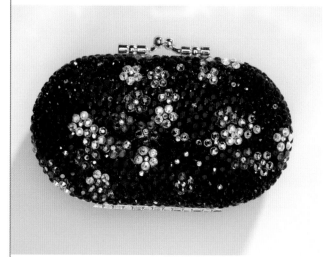

Blinged!

54

Curved Shell
Coin Purse

Objective:

 To use natural materials, in this case a cowrie shell coin purse, to recreate a pattern from nature; to fit crystals around a curved object; and to convert the small purse to an elegant purse, complete with a tassel and wrist strap.

According to Enid Nemy's "Judith Leiber: The Artful Handbag," Ms. Leiber's greatest challenge was working with natural shells. Due to the fragile nature of the material and the fact that no two are exactly alike, it proved to be quite difficult to make a limited edition of a particular style.

I found this cowrie shell coin purse made from two shell halves edged in brass and fitted with a wire hinge and clasp. The rich, beautiful coloration of the shell is reminiscent of an animal print. Inspired by the colors, I set out to transform the coin purse into a beautiful evening purse.

Materials

- Alcohol swab, or rubbing alcohol and cotton
- 1 gross jet black 12ss Swarovski foil-backed crystals
- 1 gross light Colorado topaz 12ss Swarovski foil-backed crystals
- 1 gross white opal 12ss Swarovski foil-backed crystals
- Gem-Tac or Jewel Bond glue
- Double 3" decorative turk knot tassels attached to at least 2 ft.-long rayon cord
- Round coin purse, preferably made of shell or with natural coloring

Ready, Set, Bling!

1. Clean the purse with alcohol.

2. Following the coloration of the shell, apply the crystals. Try to keep the stones as close together as possible in an alternate row pattern. On a flat surface, this is much easier to accomplish; working on a curved surface is challenging. You will be able to start out placing the crystals directly next to each other, but as you navigate the curve, the area of the shell gradually decreases, and crystals of the same size will not fit in the space you would think they should. Since the entire surface is curved, you will need to make constant adjustments. It is best to cover a small section at a time, starting from one spot and radiating out from there until the entire surface is covered.

3. To create the wrist strap, first wrap adhesive tape around the center of the rope to prevent fraying after cutting. Cut the cord in half, leaving two tassels each attached to approximately 1 ft. of cord. Put one tassel aside for another project.

Before

Blinged!

Step 4

4. Run the cord through the wire hinge on the bottom edge of the purse, leaving 1-½" of cord above the tassel to allow it to dangle freely. Take the cut end of the cord and loop it through the hinge again, going through the hinge in the same direction as the first. Take the end and loosely wrap it around the cord loop 2 to 3 times, making sure that the wraps are next to each other.

5. Run the tape-wrapped end down through the wraps ending with a small stub of cord showing. You need just enough to grab and hold while securing the knot.

6. There are now 2 strands of cord forming the loop coming out from the top of the triple wrap. One strand will pull the tassel end, reducing the length of cord dangling the tassel. The other strand when pulled will tighten the knot you have just wrapped. Pull this strand until the wraps tighten around the strap securely.

7. Put one dab of clear glue into each end of the knot after cutting the taped end flush with the wraps. Allow the glue to dry thoroughly.

8. To remove any kinks in the cord, wet the cord with water and hang from a knob or hook until dry.

Unforgettable
Perfume Atomizer

Objective:

To create a beautiful accessory using a spiraling striped pattern.

Perfume is so romantic. Any well-equipped lady will want to carry her favorite scent with her wherever she goes. Imagine pulling out this beautiful atomizer to dazzle your date or be the envy of your good friends! Buy refillable atomizers on eBay, or simply cover your favorite perfume bottle.

This stripe pattern is fun to use for any project.

Materials

- Alcohol swab, or rubbing alcohol and cotton
- 1 to 2 gross each of 3 coordinating colors 12ss foil-backed crystals
- GemTac or Jewel Bond glue
- Flat brush or toothpicks for spreading glue
- Glass or acrylic perfume atomizer or roll-on bottle

Ready, Set, Bling!

1. Starting at the base, glue rhinestones around the bottom row. Alternate 1, 2 or 3 stones of any color with varying amounts of the other colors. As you work up the case, offset one stone diagonally and follow the same pattern you've created at the base going up the side of the atomizer. Be sure to offset the same colors as the pattern progresses up the side of the bottle to produce a consistent diagonal stripe. This will become apparent to you as you work with it.

2. Glue some stones along the cap in the same manner, and cover the top any way you please.

Glamorous
Initialed Lighter

Objective:

 To create a solid color allover pattern, maintaining straight lines and an even look throughout the piece.

Although I am a non-smoker, I get so many requests for cigarette lighters that I searched eBay and found some retro imi-tation Zippo lighters for my customers. It's amazing what you can find if you only look!

Materials

- Alcohol swab, or rubbing alcohol and cotton
- 3 to 4 gross Siam 12ss Swarovski foil-backed crystals
- 10 to 20 light Siam 12ss Swarovski foil-backed crystals
- Gem-Tac or Jewel Bond glue
- Flat brush or toothpicks for spreading glue
- Zippo-style cigarette lighter
- ALTERNATE APPLICATION: Terrifically Tacky Tape or Wonder Tape

Ready, Set, Bling!

1. Clean the case with alcohol to remove fingerprints and oils.

2. Glue the Siam 12ss crystals to the surface of the lighter in an Adjacent grid pattern. Cover the entire surface, but leave the hinge and bottom uncovered.

3. You may choose to create an initial out of a coordinating color such as light Siam — this lighter has a V for Vicki. Place the initial on either one or both sides of the case near the bottom, between approximately the third row up and the third row in from the side.

∘ ◍◍ TIP ◍◍ ∘

Be very careful to check that the rows and columns line up. Solid colors are the hardest to use, because it is so difficult to mask errors in placement.

Updated
Vintage Compact

Objective:

To turn an antique accessory into the updated BLING found in the trendiest stores and on the arms of celebrities.

These vintage compacts are showing up accompanying A-listers as they walk the red carpet at all the best events. They can be found in vintage stores and on eBay — the search is half the fun! Designed originally to hold makeup and lipstick, many could also hold cigarettes and coins. You can replace cigarettes with money or credit cards if you don't smoke. Some compacts still have the telltale residue of antique powder makeup, and some may never even have been used at all. Frequently, there are lipstick tubes holders on the side of the case — replace the old tube with your own modern color.

This particular compact has a raised basket weave design. This gives dimension to the case and its Blinged surface.

Materials

- Alcohol swab, or rubbing alcohol and cotton
- 3 gross tanzanite 12ss Swarovski foil-backed crystals
- 2 gross crystal clear 12ss Swarovski foil-backed crystals
- 3 gross light rose 12ss Swarovski foil-backed crystals
- Gem-Tac or Jewel Bond glue
- Flat brush or toothpicks for spreading glue
- Vintage Art Deco compact

Ready, Set, Bling!

1. Clean the entire surface of the compact with alcohol.

2. Use the basket weave pattern as your guide to fill each space with a different color. If your compact does not have a basket weave grid, fold the pattern underneath as you proceed, and be careful to keep the rows straight. To make the stones fit the basket weave, an alternating grid pattern works best.

Before

Blinged!

Posh Pet Carrier

Objective:

To build a plaid pattern with crystals

What better way to show how much you love your dog and carry that "precious cargo" wherever you go than in a special pet carrier accented with dazzling crystals? The size of the carrier, even though it was designed for miniature breeds, dictated the number of crystals needed to cover the fabric surface and create the greatest impact.

The trick was to find a carrier that had a large surface of mesh with narrower strips of fabric above and below the mesh. The two straps and the stitched-down strap fabric attached to the bottom panel create a natural border, within which the crystals can be placed while still appearing to cover the greatest amount of surface without skimping. It is best to avoid the opening where the dog peeks out, because a few crystals could potentially fall off and become a choking hazard. Keep your dog safe by placing the embellishments out of his reach. Besides, for the purpose of creating the best design element, only filling the two front panels between the straps is more economical while still providing the greatest visual impact — and your dog will not love you any less for being frugal!

I planned to have a plaid pattern for this book from the start, but this particular carrier offered the ideal solution. As a perfect example of "form follows function," the inherent design of the purchased pet carrier dictated the best way to embellish it.

Materials

- 3 gross light Colorado topaz 12ss heat-set Swarovski crystals
- 2 gross jet black 12ss heat-set Swarovski crystals
- 2 gross Siam 12ss heat-set Swarovski crystals
- 1 gross clear 12ss heat-set Swarovski crystals
- Heat-set applicator
- Small fabric pet carrier
- ALTERNATE APPLICATION — use foil-backed crystals with Gem-Tac or Jewel Bond glue and a flat brush or toothpicks.

Ready, Set, Bling!

1. Adhere the stones to the fabric, being careful to keep the rows straight. If you are using plaid fabric, it may not be exactly even, as was the case in the sample. To make the finished design more uniform, use the basic layout of the plaid to make sure that the crystals in the first row are straight.

2. Once the first row has been established, use a counting method to fill in the rest of the pattern, governed loosely by the printed plaid fabric. In the sample, 5 topaz crystals fit in each corresponding topaz-colored fabric section, so this number was used throughout the pattern. Any vertical rows of red or black followed the placement of the corresponding red or black crystal on the foundation row, disregarding the actual print, which was angled across the panel.

3. Repeat the pattern in the same configuration on the other panel, disregarding what is printed on the fabric. The finished embellished panels should match for uniformity.

Before

Blinged!

⊙ ⊙⊙ TIP ⊙⊙ ⊙

This pattern can be used with any color combination of your choice on any solid color background.

SPECIAL NOTE:

I do not under any circumstance recommend making a dog collar, because the dog can scratch at the collar, loosen the stones and choke on them. The dog carrier I have included has the stones in the middle section, far out of the dog's reach. You can use a Brisk-Set or a BeDazzler, but they have sharp points that can harm your pet.

Wow-Them Wearables

Blazing Hot Sunglasses

Objective:

To cover a pair of sunglasses with crystals, avoiding the expense of designer glasses, and demonstrate that the decorating possibilities for simple accessories are endless!

You can glam your own glasses and save a bundle — and nobody will be able to tell that you made them yourself! Inexpensive sunglasses are readily available from discount stores. Get a designer pair of sunglasses for a lot less!

Materials

- Alcohol swab, or rubbing alcohol and cotton
- 1 to 2 gross 12ss light Colorado topaz Swarovski foil-backed crystals
- Gem-Tac or Jewel Bond glue
- Flat brush or toothpicks for spreading glue
- 1 pair sunglasses — preferably with a large surface to Bling!

Ready, Set, Bling!

1. Clean the sunglass frames with alcohol to remove fingerprints and oils.

2. Use the Alternate grid pattern to closely cover as much of the surface as you desire, in the design of your choice.

Ultimate BLING! Bracelet

Objective:

To use different Swarovski materials to create a magnificent bracelet without glued flat-back crystals.

This project is not for the faint of heart — the mesh is rather pricey — but it is a great way to create the ultimate instant BLING!

◦ ◦ ◉ Materials ◉ ◦ ◦ ◦

- ◉ Approximately 7" of 4-row Swarovski rhinestone mesh
- ◉ Two 5x10 mm crimp ends
- ◉ 2 jump rings and 1 lobster claw clasp
- ◉ E-6000 glue
- ◉ Pliers

Ready, Set, Bling!

1. Measure the length of mesh needed for a bracelet to fit your wrist. Don't forget to include in your measurement the length of the clasp and the jump rings added to the ends. The mesh cuts quite easily, but be sure to measure properly first.

2. Run a generous bead of E-6000 glue through the center of the crimp end.

3. Use the pliers to gently nudge one end of the mesh into place inside the crimp — it will require a bit of fitting to make it lie flat inside the crimp. Allow the glue to dry thoroughly.

3. When the glue is dry, use the pliers to crimp the finding over the mesh, securing the end of the mesh inside the crimp.

4. Repeat steps 2 and 3 for the other side.

5. Attach the lobster claw clasp to a jump ring and to the crimp. Attach a slightly larger jump ring to the crimp on the other side.

Silver Starburst Shoes

Objective:

To outline the rim and heel of a shoe, and to create a starburst pattern using progressively-sized crystals.

It's hard to find a dress shoe that is the correct size, color and heel height — and it's even harder to find one that is comfortable and affordable. At my son's wedding, I wanted something extraordinary, and a plain silver shoe (I couldn't even find a decent pair in black!) was the best I could do. I tried using shoe clips to dress them up, but the clips appeared dwarfed on the large vamp of my shoe — so I designed a crystal decoration in a starburst pattern using various sizes of crystals.

By the end of the evening, the shoes had taken a beating, but all of the crystals remained intact!

● ●● Materials ●● ●

- 2 gross clear 20ss foil-back Swarovski crystals
- Less than 1 gross clear 12ss foil-back Swarovski crystals
- Less than 1 gross clear 10ss foil-back Swarovski crystals
- Less than 1 gross clear 7ss foil-back Swarovski crystals
- Gem-Tac or Jewel Bond Adhesive
- Flat brush or toothpicks for glue application
- Silver closed-toed shoes

Ready, Set, Bling!

1. Glue large crystals around the rim of the shoe and the top of the heel.

2. Use gradually decreasing sizes of crystals to apply the starburst pattern, working out from the center front of each shoe.

3. Compare both shoes to be sure the crystals are applied evenly.

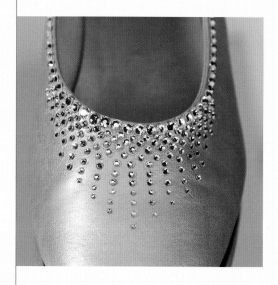

Bow Barrette

Objective:

To use alternative materials — in this case, a pretty pink appliqué designed for sewing — and imagination to create multi-dimensional Bling!

Bling hair ornaments are very popular, and they frame the face beautifully. Create your own barrette, and you will feel like a queen wearing a crown!

There are many beautiful appliqués available in the notions departments of fabrics and craft stores. Barrettes are available in any drug or variety store.

Materials

- 2 gross light rose 12ss Swarovski foil-backed crystals
- Purchased bow appliqué designed for sew-on or glue-on garment application
- Small barrette in a color to coordinate with the appliqué
- GemTac or Jewel Bond glue
- Flat brush or toothpicks for spreading glue
- ALTERNATE APPLICATION — use heat-set crystals and a heat-set applicator.

Ready, Set, Bling!

1. Glue stones all over the appliqué in any pattern, or follow the outline of the appliqué.

2. Glue the completed appliqué to the barrette, and allow it to dry thoroughly.

Beautiful Lace Shawl

Objective:

To create Bling on draped fabric.

Whether it is vintage or modern, black or colored, enhancing a lace shawl with crystals makes it so much more enchanting.

◦ ❂❂ Materials ❂❂ ◦

- ❂ 5 gross clear 20ss Swarovski heat-set stones
- ❂ 5 gross clear 12ss Swarovski heat-set stones
- ❂ Heat-set applicator
- ❂ Flat brush or toothpicks for spreading glue
- ❂ Lace shawl
- ❂ ALTERNATE APPLICATION: Use foil-backed stones and Gem-Tac or Jewel Bond glue.

Ready, Set, Bling!

1. Fill the flower buds and other solid areas in the lace with crystals. Use larger crystals for larger areas and smaller crystals elsewhere.

High-Tech Toys

Encrusted iPod Case

Objective:

To Bling an iPod case with crystals, making it even more stylish and trendy.

A search on eBay will yield a variety of metal iPod cases in all sizes and colors, including silver, black, gold, green, blue and pink. Shortly before starting this project, I found a metal case that perfectly coordinated with my beautiful pink stones. The case was purchased for a commission on my eBay site — until the customer decided that the expense was beyond her budget. This is all the more reason to embellish one for yourself — you can save the additional labor expense and gain the satisfaction of knowing that you did it yourself!

I prefer to use a pattern where every other stone is the alternate color — in this case, Lt. Rose alternating with Rose. This will help mask any irregularity in application. Straight lines are crucial, yet they are sometimes difficult to maintain over the entire project; alternating colors can compensate somewhat. Be sure to use a metal version and not one of the silicon rubber "skins" available, as the stones and glue will not adhere to them.

Materials

- Alcohol swab, or rubbing alcohol and cotton
- 3 to 4 gross light rose 12ss Swarovski foil-backed crystals
- 3 to 4 gross rose 12ss Swarovski foil-backed crystals
- 1 gross light rose 9ss Swarovski foil-backed crystals
- GemTac or Jewel Bond glue
- Flat brush or toothpicks for glue application
- Metal iPod case, sized to fit your personal iPod

Ready, Set, Bling!

1. Clean case with alcohol to remove fingerprints or other oils.

2. Work in even rows starting at one corner. Cover the edges with a single row of stones.

3. Surround the cut-out circle motif on the front with clear stones. Smaller 9ss stones cover more uniformly around the perimeter of the circle.

Dazzling
Cell Phone Case

Objective:

To add crystals to a cell phone and avoid the expense of purchasing one commercially, making this desirable item an attainable reality for any crafty "Bling-er".

Cell phone faceplates are available in mall kiosks, discount stores, and on eBay. There are faceplates to match just about any phone on the market. They usually require you to replace the one that comes with your phone by unscrewing the tiny screws under the faceplate. If you do this, keep your original faceplate to replace the one you decorate in case you have a problem with your phone — you may be voiding its warranty if you replace it.

⚬ ⚬⚬ Materials ⚬⚬ ⚬

- ❀ Alcohol swab, or rubbing alcohol and cotton
- ❀ 1 to 2 gross aquamarine 12ss Swarovski foil-backed crystals
- ❀ 1 to 2 gross tanzanite 12ss Swarovski foil-backed crystals
- ❀ 1 to 2 gross clear 12ss Swarovski foil-backed crystals
- ❀ 1 gross clear 19ss or 20ss Swarovski foil-backed crystals
- ❀ Gem-Tac or Jewel Bond glue
- ❀ Flat brush or toothpicks for spreading glue
- ❀ Cell phone faceplate

Ready, Set, Bling!

1. Clean the faceplate with alcohol to remove fingerprints and oils.

2. Using the Alternating grid pattern, cover the faceplate with the pattern of your choice. I used a harlequin pattern — however, you can use any pattern you wish. You can also use the Adjacent grid, if you wish. The choice is yours. I used the 19ss crystals to surround the circular screen. Avoid covering any of the holes that are cut into the faceplate, because they are there for a reason.

3. If your phone has a loop for a hanging cell phone dangle charm, create one to match your embellished phone.

Glittering
Tape Measure

Objective:

To work with stones and play with color possibilities.

I always carry a tape measure in my purse — you never know when you will have to get dimensions of something while out shopping — and it has come in handy many times. So, when I found this decorative keychain, I knew I had to cover it in Bling!

I selected the combination of Fuchsia and Crystal Clear AB for this project. The Crystal Clear AB stones have a distinctive pink cast to them, and alternating them with the Fuchsia in an Adjacent grid pattern allows the colors to play off of each other beautifully.

◦ ◦◉ Materials ◉◦ ◦

- ◉ Alcohol swab, or rubbing alcohol and cotton
- ◉ 1 gross fuchsia 12ss Swarovski foil-backed crystals
- ◉ 1 gross crystal clear 12ss AB Swarovski foil-backed crystals
- ◉ Gem-Tac or Jewel Bond glue
- ◉ Flat brush or toothpicks for spreading glue
- ◉ Keychain with metal-cased tape measure attached

Ready, Set, Bling!

1. Clean the tape measure keychain with alcohol.

2. Glue the stones onto the keychain, using the Adjacent pattern and alternating the fuchsia and crystal clear rhinestones.

◦ ◦◉ TIP ◉◦ ◦

If you cannot find a keychain, use a small tape measure.

Diabetes Monitor Case

Objective:

To complete a project available to all ages and price ranges while building self-esteem in a child with Juvenile Diabetes or other debilitating condition.

Juvenile Diabetes is a very difficult thing for a child to have to deal with — she must check blood sugar levels at various times of the day and take insulin, which must be administered with the assistance of school personnel. Self-esteem is important to school age children, and anything that sets a child apart from her peers is devastating. What better way to deal with this inevitability than for a young diabetic girl to decorate her own monitor or supplies case with Bling! so that she has something special for which her friends can envy her rather than tease her!

° ❀ ❀ Materials ❀ ❀ °

- ❀ Alcohol swab, or rubbing alcohol and cotton
- ❀ Assorted acrylic rhinestones
- ❀ Gem-Tac or Jewel Bond glue
- ❀ Brush or toothpicks
- ❀ Diabetes monitor case — hard shell

Ready, Set, Bling!

1. Clean the hard-shell case (do not use a fabric case) with alcohol.

2. Using an assortment of sizes and shapes of acrylic rhinestones, glue them in a random pattern all over the outside of the case. The Gem-Tac or Jewel Bond glue is water-based, so it is appropriate for a supervised project for an older child.

° ❀ ❀ TIP ❀ ❀ °

Acrylic stones can also make a good alternative for any project — and a diabetic person of any age would love to have a case as beautiful as this one!

Personalized
Puppy Lead

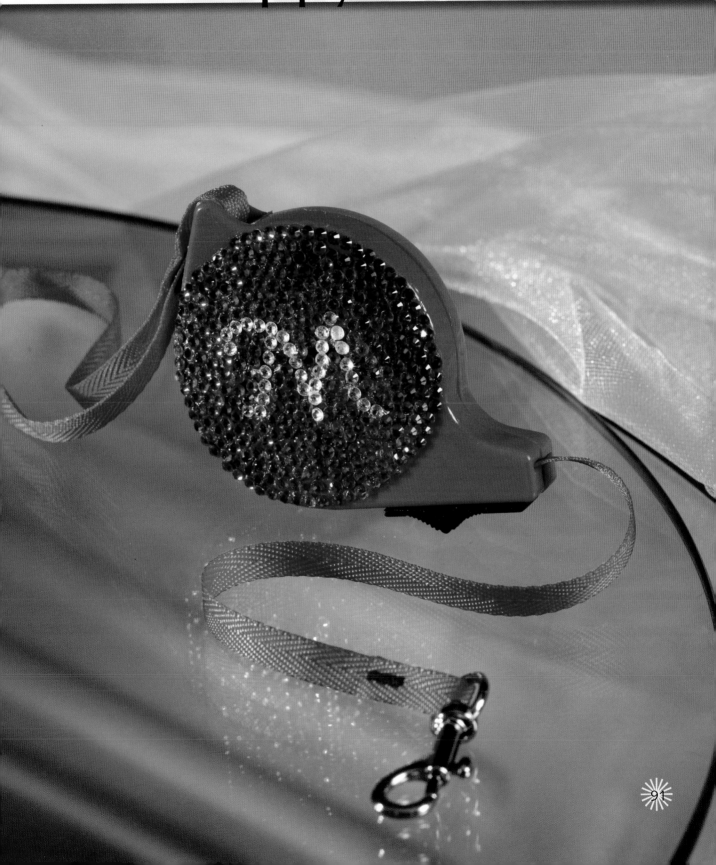

Objective:

To work with drawn initials and turn them into Bling for your dog.

While you are Blinging your personal accessories, why not add one more project to pamper your pet? Decorate one of these very popular retractable dog leads with rhinestones to show the world how special your dog is. Personalize the lead with his initial to show he's one of a kind.

This lead was created with an M for Mandy in honor of my 13-year-old English springer spaniel, who had to be put to sleep shortly before this project was finished.

❀ ❀❀ Materials ❀❀ ❀

- ❀ Alcohol swab, or rubbing alcohol and cotton
- ❀ 3 to 4 gross Siam 12ss Swarovski foil-backed crystals
- ❀ 1 gross crystal clear 12ss Swarovski foil-backed crystals
- ❀ Gem-Tac or Jewel Bond glue
- ❀ Flat brush or toothpicks for spreading glue
- ❀ Permanent pen
- ❀ Retractable plastic dog lead

Ready, Set, Bling!

1. Clean the surface of the dog lead with alcohol.

2. Draw the initial in the center of the side panel of the lead with the permanent pen.

3. Outline the initial with clear crystals.

4. Fill in the space around the letter with Siam crystals, placing them closely to leave as few gaps as possible.

5. Working in a circular pattern around the initial, fill in the entire area using Siam crystals.

About the Author

Pursuing a degree in art education led to an introduction to all aspects of crafts that Ilene loves dearly to this day.

After teaching art in Ohio, Ilene started a calligraphy magazine and met the pre-eminent American calligrapher and type designer, Arthur Baker. She is still working with him on his fonts and computer graphic interpretations of his artwork for a book on New American Calligraphy.

Ilene also designed a graphic computer program, Silver Screen Photographer, and ran a company doing children's portraits.

She designed and developed Faux Dichro, an award-winning craft product that simulates the look of fused dichroic glass. She continues to enjoy designing jewelry and exploring new crafts.

Ilene lives with her husband in Tennessee. She has two married sons and a new grandson, Garrett, the light of her life.

Resources

Suppliers

Crystals and rhinestones are available from many different craft stores, other retailers and on-line sources.

Dazzling Designs & Apparel
www.dazzlingdesignsinc.com
7001 NE 219th Street
Battleground, WA 98604
360-687-3897

eBay
www.ebay.com

Fire Mountain Gems
www.firemountaingems.com
1 Fire Mountain Way
Grants Pass, OR 97526
800-355-2137
800-423-2319

Glitz & Glamour
www.glitzonline.com
61 Betty Holland Road
Jackson, TN 38505
731-427-9116

Joyce Trimming Inc.
www.ejoyce.com
109 West 38th Street
New York, NY 10018
800-719-7133
212-719-3110

Kandi Corp.
www.KandiCorp.com
P.O. Box 8345
Clearwater, FL 33758
800-985-2634
727-441-4100

M & J Trim
www.mjtrim.com
1008 6th Avenue
New York, NY 10018
1-800-9-MJTRIM
212-204-9595

Merchants Overseas (Wholesale)
www.merchantsoverseas.com
389 Fifth Avenue
New York, NY 10016
212-594-7000
or
41 Bassett Street
Providence, RI 02903
401-331-5603

Mister Nailhead
http.stores.ebay.com/Mister-Nailhead
800-678-6808

PC Stitch
www.pcstitch.com
c/o M & R Technologies
2445 E. River Road
Dayton, OH 45439
800-800-8517

Stitch Painter
Cochenille Design Studio
www.cochenille.com
P.O. Box 235604
Encinitas, CA 92023
858-259-1698

Sue's Sparklers
www.suessparklers.com
1365 S. Juniper Street
Escondido, CA 92025

Swarovski (Wholesale)
www.swarovski.com
800-426-3088

The Rhinestone Guy
www.rhinestoneguy.com
1428 East Wilshire
Santa Ana, CA 92705
888-594-7999
714-480-1000

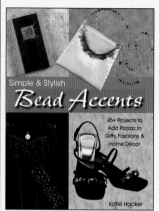

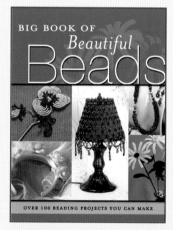

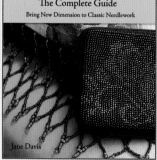